Salted With Fire

Stories and Poetry depicting the growth of
one child of God

by
Nancy LaRonda Johnson

Praise for Salted With Fire

"Johnson takes her own creations and combines them with biblical messages that should give the reader not just some enjoyment while reading but some inspiration as well. SALTED WITH FIRE is definitely a book you'll find yourself going back to." – C.A. Webb, "Conversations Book Club"

"The to-the-point flash pieces were entertaining and the poetry was beautiful. I like how this book is spiritual and uplifting." – Medeia Sharif

"All of the work here is driven by heart, and by a firm belief in God. The author is not afraid to make use of the five senses, and a full range of emotions to drive her stories." – Bonnie Cehovet

"This collection of flash fiction pieces and poetry is driven by vivid imagery, strong emotion, and faith. The stories are realistic, and some with situations I see from every day life. Some about little things, and the author manages to capture the joy in them and surprise us." – Christine Rains

Table of Contents

Author's Note

For every one shall be salted with fire, and every sacrifice shall be salted with fire. Salt is good: but if salt have lost its saltness, wherewith will ye season it? Have salt in yourselves, and have peace one with another. (Mark 9:49-50 King James Version)

A multi-interpreted verse, I see Jesus' statement as a directive that we must continually transcend ourselves to be more like him. We all go through trials, but we should never lose the "salt" or flavor that makes us who we are. Instead, through the formative forces of these trials, we must become more as God made us to be while maintaining peace in our hearts toward ourselves and each other.

This book is a representation of how this process shaped my writing. Starting from stories meant only for entertainment, my writing later expressed how I began to move toward God's outstretched hand, and ends with my desire to always write stories and poetry that depict his love, even if they are not religious in nature.

I often tell people that everything that occurs in the world, both good and evil, is in the Bible. To illustrate this, after each story is a short Biblical discussion of themes brought up in the story.

In my youth, I was fortunate to have had church as a foundation, and I have always had a strong feeling of God in my life. My favorite books at that time were a ten volume set of Bible stories. Yet, it took decades to understand how much God was with me and loved me, even while I yearned to know who he was during my difficult pre-teen and rebellious teen years.

Writing, however, was a good way for me to look into myself and give those confusing emotions a voice. Journaling thoughts, goals, dreams and poetry helped to keep me sane, as they were an outlet for the turmoil that raged within. Story writing came later, along with my interest in reading books that were too adult for my young, impressionable mind, including the sexually explicit books by Jacqueline Susan and Harold Robbins, the violent worlds created by Mario Puzo, and the salacious and entitled lives of Sidney Sheldon's characters. Still, the creative flame was lit, a flame ignited long ago by God and that is still being stoked by him.

My understanding of God's will for me as a writer has been long-coming. My endeavors into story writing were first represented by developing the craft, including expounding on emotion, creating a concise storyline, fine-tuning dialogue and, of course, the never-ending journey of grammar and flow. Despite the technical part of it, creating lives in stories was magical and fun.

Then came God's nudging me to write for his honor. This meant writing stories that bring people a greater understanding of his love, of life and of others. Although my writing often has a dark edge to it, I believe God allowed me to develop that interest to reach those who otherwise would steer clear of Christian theology.

I am still God's work in progress. This book, with its myriad of short fiction pieces (called flash fiction) and poetry, is a journey of my growth as a storyteller and sometimes poet. Starting from writing what was for pure enjoyment, to me opening my ears to God's directives, later came my desire to write about God's influence in the lives of those who reach out to him.

As a growing child of God, I am constantly salted with fire, for he never fails to mold me into who I am meant to be – someone who pleases God.

~ An Opening Verse ~

God's Always

A tear rolls down a child's face
and an unseen hand wipes it away.
A voice whispers to her heart,
"Know I am always with you."
Strength develops within and carries her
through the enemy's desire to crush her spirit.

Tears stream down a young woman's face
and an unseen hand wipes them away.
A voice whispers to her heart,
"I am with you always."
Resolve holds firm and she carries on
despite walking on the edge of the enemy's will.

Profound frowns crease a woman's brow
and an unseen hand smooths them away.
A voice whispers to her heart,
"You will know my love is yours always."
Struggles continue and she pushes through,
feeling an unknown presence stronger than the enemy's.

Hope brightens the woman's face.
Hands she now knows applaud her growth, and
His voice whispers to her heart,
"I am always with you, my love is yours always,
and your faith honors me."
Storms test, shape and strengthen her.
Yet, she will overcome and live eternally
in the presence of God,
who is with her always.

A CHILD OF THE WORLD

The stories and poems in this section
Come from my worldly joy of
Creating lives on a blank page, and were
Written only for the pure fun
Of that creation.

Too Bad! Too Late!

Laura didn't want to get up this morning. Something inside told her to pull the covers over her head and deal with calling in sick later. Her pain was waning, however, and she had already missed three days of work. With a feeling of ambivalence, Laura pushed away the covers and got out of bed.

She walked to the closet to see what suited her fancy for the day. She flipped through various colored suits and dresses until her fingers scraped against something hard and knobby.

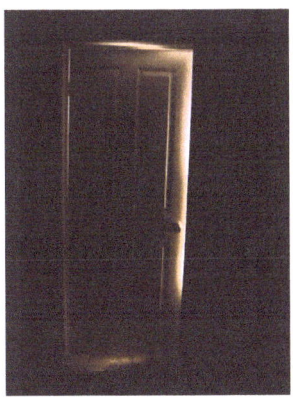

Quickly pulling her hand away, Laura retreated from the closet. She inched closer and slowly lifted a hand in between the clothing where her fingers hit the *thing*. Her hand disappeared between the items, but she felt nothing out of the ordinary. Pulling her hand back, it hit on something hard and smooth, like a stick or…. With a shriek, she exclaimed, "It's a bone. A rib bone!"

She held back a scream and spread apart the clothing. Facing her, and seeming to glare at her, was a full-on skeleton. Laura forced herself to look closer, her head straining to get nearer while her body remained far from the closet. The skeleton looked fresh and strong.

Suddenly, recognition hit her, and she laughed with a full-body guffaw. She fell backward, laughing, and landed on her bed, peering between teary blinks at the skeleton.

"You damned fool, Luis!" Laura fought to take control of her laughter, stood and walked over to the skeleton. "I told you not to come back here! You're gone and you're gone for good."

Quickly dressing in jeans and a blouse, she yanked the skeleton down, breaking the tie connecting the head to the clothing pole. She carried the skeleton to the trunk of her car; it wasn't too heavy, since Luis was only 5'5".

Laura stood looking at the skeleton she had thrown into the trunk, and said, "I told you too many times that I'd get the best of you if you didn't stop harassing me, Luis."

She slammed the trunk closed and rushed to the driver's seat. Clicking on her seatbelt, she peered through the rearview mirror, and imagined the deep-set sockets of Luis' vacant eyes staring back at her. "I gave you so many chances, but you never believed me."

Luis' menacing, dark shadow-eyes glowered at her in the mirror. Unperturbed, Laura said, "It only took one black eye from you to know exactly where I needed to go."

She started the car and drove on with Luis glaring at her from the mirror. "After you were gone," she told him, "Anita said you might try and come back, but I didn't believe her."

Luis' scowl remained on his hardened, pale skull. Unrebuffed, Laura took the turns she made every day to get to work, except for one short detour. The smell hit her before she saw the mounds of trash rising above the rooftop of the office building.

Continuing her conversation, she calmly stated, "Still, I paid attention to Anita when she told me what to do if you did return."

Following Anita's detailed instructions, Laura drove to a back lot and parked where she could see thick blooms of smoke rising from the furnace.

She felt much better than when she first awoke, and said in a commanding voice, "I know you didn't believe in black magic before, but I see you do now. Too bad, too late! The incinerator will be the end of you."

Laura waited to ensure the deed was done and that every part of the skeleton was gone for good before returning to the car. While driving to work with a smile on her face, she said to herself, "Guess it was good for me to get out of bed today."

Discussion

Years ago, I was curious about ghosts, divinations of spirits and other forms of witchcraft. I never cared to practice these mediums, as I understood that there existed a supernatural, evil power. In my youth, I had seen movies like *The Omen* and *The Exorcist*, and never desired to wander into that realm. I only wanted to know about it, a curiosity stemming from wanting to know what else was in the world other than what was before my eyes.

In the Bible, there are indications that ghosts do exist. The disciples on a boat in the middle of the Galilean Sea were afraid when Jesus walked on water toward them one night, thinking he was a ghost. (Matthew 14:22-26) Furthermore, in 1 Samuel 28, Saul requested a diviner from Endor to conjure up the ghost of Samuel to get word from God regarding an impending Philistine attack.

Ghosts and other spirits exist, even if as Christians we should leave the spirit world to God.

Secondary Illness

There was no one around. That was the only clue that yelled at her, "Turn around and get the F--- out of here!" But Jasmine suffered from attention deficit disorder. She barely heard her own thoughts, much less clues from a distant mind. That she was one day and two hours late, and had to pry open a sealed but unlocked window to enter, was a symptom of her other disorder – schizophrenia.

She convinced herself that they were hiding or had left early so she would stop being a part of their club. But she had to see what she missed so when it was her time to share, she wouldn't be totally embarrassed. Jasmine was also very low in self-esteem. Although hefty and beautiful, with big hazel eyes, thick lashes and the smoothest and darkest skin in the club, she nonetheless felt her brain was her only asset.

After entering through the window, she viewed five pillows in a circle on the living room floor, with five bodies lying on them. Jasmine couldn't believe it. Not only were they hiding from her, they were pretending to be asleep so she would leave. Anger welled inside. She had to do something. Outwardly calm, inside she stormed to the center of the circle and withdrew the prop for her performance.

She erupted in a vocal serenade of rage and twirled with energetic grace. Startled awake, the group could only stare in awe as Jasmine continued her momentous performance entitled, "The Dance of Acceptance or Death."

Feeling she had been rejected, her finale was a swerving of her sword, first in the air, then wider and lower until it sliced through the entranced audience. Warm, swirling red liquid sprayed Jasmine as she spun. With a final slash and arcing of her torso, she impelled the sword in the center mat and yelled, "As you have decided, the answer is Death!"

Jasmine slid to one knee and let the sword fall to her side, her glistening body swooping to the floor beside it. She fell fast asleep, failing to notice that her group met one day and two and a quarter hours earlier and two blocks down the street, and oblivious to the sign at the front door reading, "Relaxation: The Calming of Effects of Meditation – noon to 1:00 p.m."

IN SESSION

Discussion

This story was written only for the fun of a story and not meant to promote the stigma against mentally disabled persons.

There are a myriad of Biblical stories of people acting out of insane rage as well as paranoia, undoubtedly caused by mental disorders. King Herod immediately comes to mind. Immensely powerful, he put his mark on much of that part of the world with his magnificent edifices. Yet, he was cruel and paranoid, killing all male children two years of age and younger in order to end the threat to his kingship: Jesus, the King of Jews. (Matthew 2). There are other historical accounts of King Herod's acts stemming from fits of jealousy, paranoia and rage, even against his wife and children.

There was also King Saul. He so hated David, his son's best friend, because he was God's chosen to rule. "The next day an evil spirit from God came forcefully on Saul. He was prophesying in his house, while David was playing the lyre, as he usually did. Saul had a spear in his hand and he hurled it, saying to himself, 'I'll pin David to the wall.'" (1 Samuel 18:10-11 New International Version) Saul pursued David for years in attempts to kill the chosen king.

Sometimes You Get Shot

If you're crossing the road at a moment that a drive-by shooting occurs, you might wonder if you'll get shot. That's not a crazy concern to have, unlike when you happen to drop by a long-lost lover's home just to see if what you heard is true, that, you know, if he's married and has kids. You may think that it's highly unlikely you might get shot at that moment.

You might be thinking that it would be good to catch up on old times, to see how much he's changed, and to see if he'll recognize you because you know you've changed a heck of a lot. You never considered the possibility that you'd start off where you ended. You don't even want to think that far back. Not really. You're not thinking about how you ended, you throwing his shoes at his head and him telling you he can't help it if he's not in love with you enough to marry you.

At a drive-by, if you hear shots whizzing closer and closer to you, you know to run in the opposite direction, duck, cover and scramble out of the way in any way you can. That's normal and no one would question your reaction. However, say you're sitting on this long-lost lover's bed and you're thinking maybe something can work out here. He's giving you that look you haven't seen in forever and, even though he has the ring on and pictures of the two kids and the little lady on the nightstand, you consider what might happen. In that moment, getting shot never pops up in your mind.

When the two of you are getting hot and heavy – this is after he's already explained to you how everyday he's thinking of a way to get out of his marriage – you get the image in your mind that you are exactly like you were way back when. Your blood flows like then, you imagine the kisses with the same passion, and you tell yourself your body feels the same way it did then.

Things are so good, nothing else comes to your mind. There are no rationalizations about what you're doing or who might get hurt, because your mind is stuck back in those far away times. You're not thinking about how he slipped the ring off his hand or how he happened to upturn the pictures on his nightstand. All you're thinking about is how his lips and tongue feel good on yours, and how his hands can get to so many places on your body so fast and so good.

He's also told you how his kids are old enough to know that things need to end between him and his wife, and that they know everyone would be better off. Even so, you don't go near to telling him that you also had to get away from yours. There's no chance you can tell him that your man has been following you, insistent on not letting things end the way they inevitably will.

No, when you're in the moment, not thinking of consequences or how you'll feel afterwards, you're only thinking about how good you feel at that time, and you don't realize that the time will not last. You don't admit that the excitement you're feeling and the thoughts that took you back to those far away times are temporary, much more so than you can comprehend. Because, although there is no drive-by and you're not hearing bullets blow past you and you're not running in the opposite direction, you are nonetheless blown back when your man, who followed you every step of the way, only needs time enough to make sure you will not leave the house having done nothing with your long-lost.

No, he waits long enough and listens hard enough until he could hear the moaning and pants of your passions to load his pistol and kick in the door, even though it isn't locked. Your long-lost doesn't hear the door being kicked in, he's so wrapped up in what he's doing, and he is not expecting anyone to come home in another four hours. He does hear the report of the gun, though. And after he backs up, he doesn't return to help you. He jumps up and runs in the opposite direction of the shooting, which is out the window.

Neither does your man say anything to you after he shoots you. He knows he's done his job, that the bullet will do you in in just a little while. Instead, he puts his gun away in his pants, turns and walks away the way he came in, leaving you to think that if this had been a drive-by shooting, there would have been multiple shots and you could have run away, a natural reaction to being placed in danger. When you didn't know that your man had even followed you while you went to see about this long-lost love, and you didn't consider that something other than a catch up of lives would happen, you don't think that someone might get hurt.

When your lights are starting to fade out, the question comes to you that if you knew this was going to happen would you have still left? But it never occurred to you that in this situation, just like in a drive-by shooting, sometimes you just might get shot.

Discussion

My intent for this story was to look into the mind of someone who ends up in an unplanned, compromising position and the consequences that come from that act. Please do not think that I am blaming the woman for her ex's act of murder. This is one outcome of someone who has acted without considering her motives or consequences.

In the Bible, there were people also who behaved in ways without considering the consequences of their actions, causing devastating results. When David remained in his palace instead of taking part in a battle, he noticed Bathsheba bathing on her roof, and lust took hold of him. A king after God's heart, King David nonetheless committed the grievous sin of adultery. Once David learned that Bathsheba was pregnant, he attempted to conceal his adultery and the resulting pregnancy by sending Bathsheba's husband to her. A faithful warrior, the husband refused to lie with his wife. So David went further and committed murder by sending Bathsheba's husband into the front lines so he would be killed in war. (2 Samuel 11)

Still loved by God, David did not go unpunished. The child from his sin became ill and died. Yet, David accepted his punishment and returned to faithfully serving God. (2 Samuel 12)

death of a savior

the chair sits me upon it
– a wooden friend to my worn flesh.
    i let them inhabit me:
bugs weave through my hair (and warm my scalp),
beetles scuttle under my shirt,
slugs take over my legs (and slicken them),
spiders web me once over (insistent on preserving me),
    -- the impossibility.
    ants trudge across my body (a new frontier),
and flies land on me, and birds splatter me,
and the dog tears at my shoes and jumps
on my lap (my continual, destructive friend).

    the chickens cheep their hunger to me,
but my ears are the homes of moths,
my eyes food for the spiders,
my nose caves to worms, and
my mouth has been sucked dry.

    my flesh becomes petrified, and
my feet are roots.
    my back clings to the chair that sat
me upon it, and it too turns to moss.
    i am no longer of the human life,
and am desecrated only by insects.

    my flesh is no longer flesh,
my mind no longer minds, and
my heart no longer feels.
    but the chickens continue to cheep,
and the dog barks across my land.
    the sun continues to shine on my world,
and rain feeds us all.
    i harken to no one,
and responsibility is no longer mine.

Debt

My mind focused on the multiplying beads of sweat running down my forehead, each one trying to reach my chin first. Sal was going to come any minute, too soon to conjure up some excuse as to why I had to leave without making a payment toward what I already owed him, a measly $500.

This was his fault. Why the hell would he have me

come here? He knew I would not be able to resist a touch and pull of the arm, or the sounds and flashing of lights. He knew that would lead me to the tables, where even he had

banished me from going near! Not really banished, but he urged me with that all-knowing and mockery-driven sneer that made his sagging jowls and baggy eyes jiggle to the point where they looked to be laughing at me. Nothing about him would be laughing once he heard about the $50,000 I lost tonight.

I had to tell him! It was as simple as that. But it wasn't simple according to my gut, which lurched and jostled as if I were being dangled from the roof of that building, the one that Justin texted me from only hours before his body was found at the bottom of at four o'clock in the morning.

This time I did too much. Sal would kill me. I had to use my silver tongue like I'd never done before. I'd have to talk with a golden voice. I would convince Sal that this was his fault, and it wouldn't seem like I was shirking my responsibility.

As Sal walked up, I drew my soaking napkin across my forehead one more time, and I did it. My tongue was smooth, with just the right amount of silkiness and whine. The words I spoke were like they came directly from God, and I saw Sal's eyes soften. Instead of the two pistols pointing at me from his beady eyes like before my eloquent monologue, his eyes looked milky and glossed over with emotion.

When I finished, I swore he was silent for nearly an hour. Then he grumbled out, not in anger, not with mockery, but with an air of mercy, "I see what you're saying. You're right; I shouldn't have had you come here. To tell you the truth, I don't know why I did. Guess I was busy and not thinking."

He placed his hands over his paunch, which wasn't that big, but had a suitable ledge for him to rest his hands when he didn't want them hanging to his sides uselessly. "I'm thinking now," he said. "This is what I'll do for you, and you've got exactly one minute to decide. My youngest daughter is looking to marry. She's got the perfect guy picked out and can't wait. But I'm from the old school and will not marry her off until her older sister is married first."

I felt my legs wobble and my body began to sink toward the ground. Sal looked to his stooges, who lifted me up. Everyone knew Sal's oldest daughter. Notorious Natalie was what most called her. Notorious Natalie was supposed to have been married five years ago, but when the unlucky bastard talked too long to one of the beautiful patronages at the roulette table, Natalie beat him to unconsciousness with her hefty size eleven spiked shoes. Sal waited until the poor sap woke up before tossing his, *then*, no-longer-living body into a ditch. That was the first. There had been two others since.

"Marry her tomorrow and all is forgiven. Otherwise you have to pay me by midnight tonight." Seeing the fear and near delirium in my eyes, he added, "The wedding will happen, and you will be safe. I guarantee it."

Maybe the wedding would happen, but I'd never be safe again. I began to list in my head the names of towns and banks outside of Sal's domain. I knew I could do a bank job and pay Sal my $50,500 debt well before midnight. Or I'd die trying.

Discussion

Here is a wonderful verse of the Bible for those to whom money is owed: "The rich rule over the poor, and the borrower is the slave to the lender." (Proverbs 22:7 New International Version) By this, God is saying debt will make the borrower a servant to those they owe.

Yet, God does believe in forgiving debt in certain cases, thus the parable of the unmerciful servant. (Matthew 18:21-35) When a servant could not pay the king's debt, the king ordered the servant to sell his children and all that he owned to pay off the debt. The servant begged on his knees for the king to have mercy and patience. The king took pity on him and cancelled the debt.

The servant left and saw a fellow servant who owed him money. When the friend was unable to pay the debt, the servant grabbed him and choked him, demanding payment. The friend begged on his knees for mercy and patience until he could pay the debt off. The servant, however, refused and went to throw the friend into prison until the debt could be paid.

When the king heard of the servant's behavior, he summoned him, called him a "wicked servant," and reminded him how he was shown mercy. The king then threw the servant into prison to be tortured until the full debt could be paid.

The point of the parable isn't that debt is sin, but that if you do not forgive from your heart, God will also not forgive you. A much scarier thought than marrying Notorious Natalie.

Birthdays

It's something not to talk about,
given that most times I see myself as I was
and not as I am.

People come in and say,
"Ah! Happy birthday, young lady!"
and I wish I could spit at them.
If I wanted to celebrate
my birthday
with anyone other than myself
I'd be on Facebook.

Instead, I try my best to stay within,
isolated,
dreaming of all the ghosts of my past,
remembering the true birthday celebrations of
my youth.

At this point,
birthdays are a commemoration of
approaching death.
Why would I want people to say
in essence,
their true words of,
"Happy near death! Look at you
knocking on death's door. God bless you!"?

I'd like to say to them,
"Stop letting the Grim Reaper
know I'm so close!"

What I grumble instead,
while waving them away is,
"Truck it all to h...."

Career Day

"Everyone welcome Debbie's mother, Mrs. Redwood. She has a magnificent job that I am sure each of you will be thrilled to hear about. This will be a big surprise, since Debbie is new here and I doubt anyone knows what her mother does for a living. I will give you one hint: Every night when you fall asleep, Mrs. Redwood could tell exactly what you are dreaming of! Now listen closely."

Mrs. Stinson scuttled to her desk to listen attentively to Margaret Redwood's presentation. After hearing about the tedious lives of office managers, construction workers and a book editor, she could not wait for this.

Looking haggard, Debbie's mother, Margaret, languidly made her way to the front of the class. Her listless demeanor gave Mrs. Stinson immediate concern. Since Margaret had just made it to the class, Mrs. Stinson only had the opportunity for a quick greeting. Seeing how flaccid Margaret appeared now, Mrs. Stinson wished she had talked to her more.

Margaret leaned against the podium at the front of the classroom, slowly scanned the students, and finally spoke. "If you ever have to do this for your child, get out of it at every cost." She tapped her long, manicured nails against the base of the podium. "I really hate speaking in front of people...in front of crowds. I never do it. Never!"

Her embarrassed blushing darkened the creaminess of her brown skin and made her look feverish. She stammered, "W-what...I...do.... What...I...used to do…until today….″ She looked to the floor, then back to the dismayed third graders. "I hate it. I just hate it!"

With that, Margaret slid to the floor and bawled, her head bouncing on folded knees in rhythm to her cries. Lifting her head, she whimpered, "I got fired. Just yesterday I found out. Of all the jobs, I'd never worked as hard or loved as much as this one. And now I've got nothing."

Margaret covered her head again, and Mrs. Stinson finally gathered herself enough to try and take control. She wanted to dismiss the class, but it was too soon for recess. She looked to the teacher's pet and said, "Amanda, hurry and get the Assistant Principal. We need to dismiss the class."

A roar of cheers soared through the classroom as nearly every child stole gleeful glances at Margaret's pathetic form balled up on the floor. Then Desmond, the brainiac of the classroom, stood, pounded his book on his desk, and yelled, "Just wait a minute! I need to know one thing." Quiet settled over the room as everyone beheld the usually timid Desmond looking much more determined and grown up than his eight years.

"Before we leave," he stepped closer to Margaret Redwood and looked directly into her eyes, "I want to know what-the-heck-job you used to have!"

All the students kicked up a fuss and hurled wadded papers at Desmond. Margaret Redwood cried even louder, putting end to Career Day.

Discussion

With public speaking being the number one fear, it is no surprise that major Biblical figures also held that fear. God called on Moses to free the Israelites from their Egyptian oppressors. (Exodus 4) Unfortunately for Moses, that meant speaking to the Pharaoh on the Israelites' behalf. This was something that horrified Moses, who feared public speaking to the point that he doubted God for giving him this charge.

Although God would have given Moses the abilities he needed, being an understanding and faithful God, he allowed Moses' brother Aaron to speak for him.

Even the Apostle Paul, the most evangelical Christian, had doubts and insecurities of his speaking abilities. Paul, however, believed in the message he had to relay. He trusted God's will and worked hard to fulfill his public speaking duties. (2 Corinthians 11:6)

You Are Not Going To Believe This

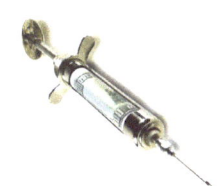

"You're not going to believe this, but…"

"Sir." A rusty croak of a sound emitted from the nurse, who was old enough that she must have been working when nurses used to wear those white hats that resembled sailors' caps. Her wrinkled and not-so-pale as much as ashen face slowly lifted to see me looking desperately at her.

My desperation, I wanted to ensure her, was nothing less than me needing to impress upon her how down-right honest I was being. "Just last year I was supposed to go out of the country…"

"Sir." The sound again. It was raking to my ears and I had to stop her from saying another word. She had to hear, actually listen, to what I was saying anyway.

"Not to just any country, but one where you had to take all the shots imaginable in order to purchase a ticket. You know, third world? Really, closer to fourth world."

She cut me off and I geared myself, not wanting to be so rude as to cover my ears from her grating vocal sounds. "You've got to get this done."

I almost wanted to give in just to not hear her again. But, I couldn't. Barely taking a deep enough of a breath to get it all out, I quickly blurted, "Just last year, they had to send me to the emergency room. My reaction was almost fatal. My body swelled; I looked like a sumo wrestler. My skin, already dark, as you can see – I've tracked my lineage to Africa, a northern region you probably never heard of – went charred. You'd think my uncle had left me on the grill for as long as he'd left the hot dogs on Memorial Day. You couldn't even eat them. I bit one without looking at it and threw up black chunks of ash and burnt flesh."

"Mr. Talè!"

She'd cut me off again. I could not accept that and looked at her with such consternation that she reeled backward a little. Being as old as she was, I felt the need to steady her to make sure she didn't stumble and break most of her bones, but I was making a point. Stressing each word with harsh chastisement, I said, "You've got to understand, if you put that thing in me, I will die."

She took another step back. Thrilled that I put her on the defensive, I continued in a quickened prattle, "Like I said, last year, you could look it up in my records, just call my doctor. But last year, the ambulance came rushing with lights flashing and sirens blaring. My mom flew in from New Jersey. You know how long that took? It was my mom who first said, 'Under no circumstances must you ever get a shot. Not even a flu shot.' Then my doctor said the same thing – the emergency room doctor. And even my general practitioner gave me that undisputable command."

I ran out of breath and the nurse took up her offense so quickly I could do nothing, not even guard myself against her onslaught of vocal blitzing. "What your records do say, Mr. Titan Talè, is that you have a very serious illness that you may have been prone to since birth."

"You are so right!" I had her now. She was talking sense, while at the same time nearly shattering me with the screeching coming from her mouth. "But you probably don't know my other condition. Certain sounds can send me to the emergency room too, because they can cause me to have seizures. That's not as uncommon as it seems. It's even been on the news and joked about on sitcoms. So, please don't talk anymore. You seem to understand why that thing in your hand can't come near my body. And if you say anything more, I'll go into convulsions."

Incredulously, she didn't get it. In an even louder and shriller voice, which scraped against my soul as well as my eardrums, she said, "Hypochondria is a very serious condition. You should really go see your psychiatrist. Our notes show that you haven't seen him in a year. If you don't control your disorder, it can make you believe you're so sick that you can cause your injuries to actually happen. This flu shot is necessary for you to continue in your job."

Before she even finished talking, she shot me in one of my arms, both of which were taut from the grip of my hands on the examination table. As she continued talking, I felt myself begin to judder like the engine in my first Oldsmobile. Then the effect of the shot took hold and I felt my body expanding.

The nurse shrieked, rushed forward and tripped over my feet while I was falling off the table. The convulsions were getting more acute and my body was swelling to twice its size.

Amongst it all, right before passing out with the nurse collapsed between my enlarging and quivering arms, I was able to eke out, "And that's why I can no longer get flu shots."

Discussion

There was a woman with an issue of blood, in that she had a medical-based bleeding problem which she suffered with for twelve years. Doctors could do nothing to relieve her suffering. Her hopelessness and frustration could hardly be imagined when you consider that every time she must have gone to the doctor for treatments, they consistently failed. It could even be believed that the doctors may have blamed her for the disorder.

When Jesus, a renowned healer who had shown compassion and provided cures to so many arrived in town, no one was going to deny her access to him. With complete faith, the woman knew if she could only touch the hem of his garment she could be cured.

Often times, a patient knows what treatment is best for her. Indeed, the strength of the woman's faith even surprised Jesus, for he felt power leave him at her touch.

But what if Jesus had denied her access? You can almost imagine an even sadder result than that of the satirical episode of Mr. Titan Talé.

The complete story of the woman with the issue of blood is found in Matthew 9:20-22, Mark 5:25-34 and Luke 8:43-48.

Strange

Strange that with all there is to see,
with continual movements,
with sounds which never cease,
with emotions that flow through
the atmosphere like wandering spirits;

Strange that with skin that feels incessantly,
with life all around,
with the air that blows for everyone,
even for those who are suffocating;

Strange that with people still creating,
not just life but stories and paintings and music,
with death permeating the world,
with eyes lurking around to see what everyone else sees,
and possibly something unseen,

That so few let go…
but persistently
    move,
      hear,
        feel,
          touch,
        breathe,
      create,
    and search…
while the heart tries to find a moment of silence,
while the body pushes its way to a point of stillness,
and the mind, facing complacency,
stands at the edge of solitude.

Homeless

I wonder what it would be like to give up my home
– to roam around the state, country, continent and farther
without a base in my mind to where I could return.

A different sort of homelessness;
one in which I couldn't even claim a city when asked,

> "Where do you stay?"
> "My home," I would say, "is this planet."

My new identity would be my domicile – nomad.
I am nomad without a habitation,
without a connection to my foundation.
I explore different parts of the world,
encountering beings new and different from me.

Then, I expect, my whole self would change,
be transformed, even from that identity as nomad.

BECOMING TRANSFORMED

A desire has been lit
For me to write in a way that pleases God,
Not only by writing Christian fiction,
But by writing stories and poetry
That bring light to who he is
And who he wants us to be.

You Wanna Be a Funambulist?

(Try to guess the meaning of funambulist from the story. The definition is at the end.)

"Have you ever been trained as a funambulist?"

"Well, not really."

I saw the interviewer blanch, and added, "It came natural." I shifted in my seat, and straightened up; this was an interview, after all. "I came from a long line of funambulists. A very long line."

"Still, there is quite a liability issue."

"Think of it this way, would you need to ask a frog whether it had been trained to hop onto a lily pad?" He smirked and was about to say something. I quickly continued, "Or a bumble bee what training he had to gather pollen? Believe me, it's similar. My first steps were made on a rope stretched out on the floor. It's all videotaped." I then gave him the name – my family stage name.

With great surprise, he blurted out, "Why don't you work with your family? Why go to a competitor?"

Now I smirked, unable to stifle a small chuckle. "My family has no real competitors."

He wasn't offended, thankfully, since he had to know the truth of my statement. To answer his question, I said, "My family doesn't understand me. They don't see why I want this to be not only my career, but my enjoyment as well. They are, in essence, the opposite of gypsies and don't feel work and fun should mix. They've always said that our profession is a spelling misnomer."

The interviewer then jumped up, stuck out his hand, and said jovially, "Welcome aboard, Claude. You are our new funambulist and can start after you meet the family. As you may know, we gypsies have a large family. And you can familiarize yourself with our tent and setup."

"No need. But thank you," I said shaking his hand robustly.

"Oh yeah, you're a natural!"

~   ~   ~

Funambulist: (fyoo-nam-byuh-list) (noun) a tightrope walker

Discussion

This is a story about the gifts God gives people. God does bestow gifts on everyone, believers and nonbelievers alike. The Bible is rife with talented characters. I'll only name a few here.

There was Joseph, who had the talent of interpreting dreams. In lieu of killing Joseph, his jealous brothers sold him. Joseph's talent, however, helped to promote him to second in command of Egypt, where he was initially a slave and later imprison. (Genesis 37)

There was also Daniel, whose God given gift went beyond human ability when he first had to tell King Nebuchadnezzar his own dream and then interpret it to save the wise men of Babylon from being killed. (Daniel 2:24-44)

King Herod was considered a genius in his talent of building the most elaborate structures throughout Rome and Judaea. All good things come from God, even for the unbeliever.

Taxi!

Marcus dreaded the hope he had held onto for so long. Marietta was four when Charlise took her. Now, seven years later, he doubted that he would recognize his own daughter.

An old friend of Charlise finally admitted that she had received a post card from Charlise a year ago. Using what little information he gathered from the postcard, Marcus immediately went looking, driving nonstop, to find Marietta. He barely considered that he had stolen his employer's car to do so.

To Marcus, it was much worse for his wife to steal his daughter after losing custody of her, as if it wasn't her fault she decided to live with a convicted child molester.

Marcus arrived in this godforsaken town three hours ago. He could not get himself to end his futile search and find a place to park the stolen taxi cab for the night.

His red, itchy and heavy eyes threatened to stay shut every time he blinked. Finally he noticed an open Mexican restaurant. He would park and pray that Charlise worked there. Whenever she did work, it was always as a waitress. Marcus sent a quick petition to God that he would find them.

Before turning into the parking lot, he heard a meek

yet shrill voice cry out, "Taxi!"

Marcus whipped his head around and saw a girl of at least thirteen in front of a closed library, hailing him.

His heart skipped a beat, but Marietta was only eleven, and this girl had short natural hair. Charlise would die before letting Marietta go without any type of hair straightener. Marcus had to see what this young girl needed, and hurriedly made a U-turn.

She opened the rear door, jumped in, and said, "See that Mexican restaurant across the street? In about five minutes, a man is going to come out. I want you to follow him."

Turning around to look at the girl, Marcus saw the layers of make-up and knew why he thought she looked older. His shock prevented tears from falling or his mouth from working. His vision blurred, but finally he was able to shout, "Marietta!" She looked the same after all, only her eleven-year-old body was camouflaged with makeup and clothing too old for her.

Marietta stared at him, fear spreading across her face. Then recognition formed along with tears in her eyes.

"Daddy?" She said it so softly, then louder, "Daddy!"

They hugged and kissed each other, crying as they spoke.

"They told me you didn't want me anymore."

"I've been looking for you forever," Marcus said, talking over her.

"I knew they were lying," she said before Marcus finished.

"Are you okay?" Marcus asked.

At the same time she said, "They told me that you died so I wouldn't ask to go home anymore."

With barely a break in between, Marcus said, "I was never going to stop looking for you."

After a few moments of silence, Marietta said, "Daddy, that guy who's coming out the restaurant said he's taking me to a secret place tomorrow where he will get paid to take pictures of me. I wanted to follow him and see where that secret place is so I could stay away."

Horrified, Marcus shouted, "Buckle up!"

He drove away and, on the way home, they shared every difficult moment since they last saw each other.

Two days later, after arriving home, Marcus went to the District Attorney's Office to file a report against Charlise.

Discussion

There are many stories in the Bible in which children are put at risk and even killed. Infant Moses was cast in the river to protect him when Pharaoh ordered that all first born Hebrew children be killed by drowning in the Nile river. (Exodus 1:22) In Exodus 13:15, God killed the firstborn of Egyptians and animals when Pharaoh refused to let the Israelites leave Egypt. There was also King Herod, who killed male children two and under to prevent the King of Israel, Jesus, from existing. (Matthew 2:16) Children are not free from Satan's schemes or God's wrath.

God, however, in his love and patience, gives much time and numerous warnings for people to obey him. God took the firstborn from the Egyptians only after many less devastating signs and warnings failed to persuade them to let the Israelites leave. (Exodus 6-11)

In *Taxi!*, Marietta was not killed, but she was stolen and put at risk. Once a lost one is found, as in the parables of the lost sheep (Luke 15:3-7) and the lost coin (Luke 15:8-10), there is much rejoicing by the angels of God. In the parable of the prodigal son, the son left of his own accord to do as he pleased with his inheritance even before he had the right to it. (Luke 15:11-32) Even so, for the father of this prodigal son, as for our Father in heaven and Marietta's father, the reunion was so sweet. It is even more glorious when you realize that those who were lost would likely have lost their eternal souls if they had not been found.

Freeway

Sometimes they stop coming right away. Other times I'm waiting endless hours and finally give up to sleep in the woods, if there are any, at the side of the road. Times like that can be a blessing, because I really don't want to risk going anyway. Sleeping, then, is always the best choice. It's not good to commit yourself to a plan if things aren't going right. They keep on not going right.

So, even if it's cold out, I go crawling into a bush I hope is large enough to keep me from view of any wannabe predators, curl up into a ball, fall fast asleep, and let loose my night growl, so I've been told it sounds like.

Tonight, it seems I caught my luck. Been there about ten minutes, and the last car, a Pinto believe it or not, pulls off the freeway exit and starts to slow down. As it nears and the headlights pass across and over where I stand, I freeze.

The driver, a half-way decent looking guy, reaches over, unlocks the passenger door, and gives it a nudge, letting the creaky door bounce on its uneven hinge. Before I notice her, a tall girl, a woman really, pulls on the rusted door handle, causing the door to emit a loud squawk as it opens wider.

Before getting in, she peers through the doorway, almost stooping, to see the driver, and says, "I was heading anywhere south. Going that way?"

A slight grimace comes upon his face, "Well, I'll be going that way in about an hour, if you want to tag along. Got a couple of errands to run first."

I can see she is a bit disappointed, as it has gotten darker. She probably wanted to get on her way as soon as possible, just in case this guy isn't what he seems and she might have to pull out some self-defense and start her freeway run all over again. But she puts a smile on her face and says the hitchhiker's credo, "There's no wrong way if it's eventually going my way." At least it's a philosophy I hear stated over and over again in various ways. "Guess I'd probably be out here all night waiting for another ride."

She throws her backpack in the back, crawls into the passenger seat, and noisily closes the creaky door; there is really no other way to close it.

While the Pinto pulls off the side of the road toward the freeway entrance, I make my way. In the last three days, every time I tried to go, the traffic was just way too much. Now I am free to roam alone all by myself. I creep gingerly to the center of the road, feeling liberated to wander as I please.

After shutting my eyes, I see a bright light filter through my closed lids. Just then I remember that the decent-looking driver said he had some errands to run. The vibrations tickle my feet as the car makes a sudden U-turn, and I feel the warmth and smell the exhaust of the revving engine. Unable to move, I quickly blurt out my prayer, "Well, Mom, Dad, my brothers and sisters, cousins, uncles and aunts, grandparents, and all of you I know and don't know, here I come to meet you in heaven."

Right before darkness shrouds over me, taking away any pain I might feel, I hear the tall girl, who is a woman really, exclaim, "Watch it! There's a possum in the roa…!"

Discussion

God often tries to deter us from the road we're on or from a path we're taking because the end is not what he wants for us. Unfortunately, we don't always heed his warnings, at times not realizing them as the warnings they are.

What immediately comes to mind is the story of Jonah, who heard God's voice telling him to go preach to a wicked city. (Jonah 1) Jonah, however, feared the people of that land and tried to flee from God by boarding a ship headed elsewhere. God sent a violent storm, which even the non-believers knew was from God. After learning that he was the cause of the storm, Jonah told the sailors to throw him overboard and that the waters would be stilled. Undoubtedly, Jonah and the sailors knew they were headed for death. Jonah decided to sacrifice only himself by offering to be thrown into the sea.

Unable to combat the storm, the sailors cried out to God and finally threw Jonah overboard. The sea grew calm. Of course, that was when Jonah was swallowed by the whale and spewed up where he was supposed to go initially, but only after acquiescing to God's will.

One thing about God is that he makes even our bad decisions have good outcomes. Those sailors, who initially worshipped different gods, believed in the one God after the seas calmed, and offered sacrifice to the Lord, making vows to him. (Jonah 1:16)

Taking one small step

Taking one small step,
knowing there's love at the end.
How do I endure talking?
How do I feel secure?
How do I throw away the hurts
from my youth?

Taking a big leap forward,
knowing God will not let me fall.
Will I show myself under a microscope
and fear my flaws are indelible?
Will I hide my true face,
not knowing what it looks like?
Will I let myself cry and
welcome the comforting hand of my love?

Running far ahead,
there's no fear about where I'll end.
My God will lead my love and me
on a righteous journey.
I will be embraced and will open my heart
to the bounty of love found.
I will gratify my Lord with the sacrifice
of following His will.
I will start by taking one small step.

A CHILD OF GOD REBORN

God is working his miracles.
Initially, not understanding how he
Was in my life,
I now see how I must strive
To write for an audience of one.
God must be the purpose and
Goal of why I write: to share his
Love, understanding, and
Desires for all people.

God's Universe

When God made the universe,
    He made it knowing of my existence to come.
For God made the universe from me.

When God made the universe,
        one universal molecule was my love of writing,
        this one my love of family,
        while that one my love of growth.
Thus God made the universe out of me.
For this is how He builds His love.

He lives there in me,
        knowing each of my molecules,
        and each of my loves.
And He lives,
        knowing all decisions there are for me,
        and every role I will play at each stage in my life.

When God made the universe,
        He made it knowing of my existence to come,
        knowing which of His gifts He would bestow.
And here I live with my God in His universe.

Quarter To

It was a quarter to. I wasn't going to make it. I could only hope the consequences of my failure would not be as devastating as Martin had said they would be. He was talking about something totally different. He had to, because he could not have known what this day would bring being that he died two years ago. But I couldn't deny how eerily fitting his warning was for this day:

> *Perry, this must not happen again. I was here to get you today, but I'm telling you, the next time it'll be all on you. You must adhere to time. If this happens again, all the work we've done will have been for nothing and we all will lose.*

Of course I thought Martin was being dramatic, like he could be when he had to wait on people. Only, I forgot to set the alarm again when I knew I should have, given what time I'd gotten in. Martin told me to be careful. He had been so clear. I was stupid to not listen to him. Thank God he would never know the turmoil I would cause.

Oh, I had to stop thinking like that, like it was already too late. It didn't have to be. It was a quarter to and I still had time.

I jumped out of bed and rushed to use the restroom, cursing myself for needing to waste that amount of time. The attire from last night was in the bathroom, although I didn't remember taking it off. I quickly threw it on after rinsing my hands with the *No Touch*, and ran for my shoes. My equipment was by the door, where it should have been. At least everything was prepared.

Only seven minutes had passed since waking up by the time I left my room, soon to enter the stormy gloom out there. It wasn't nighttime. Despite the pitch darkness and blusteriness, it was nearly one in the afternoon. I had less than nine minutes to get ready before I ruined everything.

Once all set, I silently made my way to the front and knew it wasn't too late. Feeling my way in the dark, the winds were just dying down by the time I reached the front line. I walked through the opening and my heart pounded against my chest, feeling near to explode. The lights came on, shining directly on me and reflecting the illuminants of my wardrobe.

I called out in a commanding voice, "Come all ye shepherds, ye children of earth, Come ye, bring greetings to yon heavenly birth."

The applause was deafening, and I continued on with the lyrics and the rest of my lines for the town's Christmas tribute.

Discussion

It is our duty to "work heartily, as unto the Lord, and not unto men", since it is the Lord who gives us our inheritance. (Colossians 3:23-24 American Standard Version).

This is a lesson I must relearn every day. It is easy to become spoiled and skirt responsibilities if there isn't someone watching over us all the time. Getting to work late, which could put others who rely on us at a disadvantage, can become one of our lackings. Some of us may be inclined to be late to just about everything, not only work.

But knowing that God sees all I do gives me the drive to act in a way which pleases him. I just have to remind myself and try to conform to his will each day.

It helps me to know that Jesus, in his youth, "grew in wisdom, stature, and in favor with God and man." (Luke 2:52 New International Version) Thus, even Jesus, the Son of God, had to spend time learning how to please God and how to relate to people in daily life. This was even more expounded in Hebrews 5:8-9, "Son though he was, he learned obedience from what he suffered and, once made perfect, he became the source of eternal salvation for all who obey him". (American Standard Version)

Braden's Pop

Henry took out a pinch of the spinach and felt like a fool. How could he even consider doing this at 43 years old? His own ten-year-old son would laugh at him and probably never see him as the hero he had before all this began. He was glad to have no choice but to send Braden away with the others, and tried to forget the tears that welled in his son's eyes.

Henry had no other options. To tell the truth, he got sick of looking for other ways out and he didn't care if he looked like a fool. He only wanted to slow his mind down for one hour and not witness his world be vanquished. Just about everyone in his small seaside town had already left. What else could he do?

Dropping the pinch of spinach back into the can, he used several fingers to grab as much of the dark green, slithery veggies he could and downed them in one gulp, barely putting forth the effort to chew. Henry forced back a gag reflex and woofed down another gob.

Before the last stringy stem slid down his throat, he felt the change happen. Stiff, short hairs began to push out on his chin, which itself jutted forward and became two mounds of tough roundness. One eye squinted, while the other popped open wide. The hair on his head disappeared and a small corn-colored pipe stuck out of his sneering mouth. Automatically, his arms swung to the side of him, their immense weight pulling his lanky torso forward as Henry charged at the oncoming brute.

"Aye, aye, aye, aye, aye," Henry laughed out loud, clobbering the hairy brute on the jaw and sending him flying out of his shoes. "And don't you come back this way again!"

Soon after, Henry's former self returned. Gone were the alien ships and the enormous and evil leader. His son Braden ran up to him, "Dad, I saw everything and you were great! You are my superhero!" By then, the townsfolk had witnessed the fleeing of the ships and began to make their way back home.

"I yam what I yam, son! No one else wanted to risk contaminating themselves with the only spinach those brutes left after gorging themselves on our greenery. Let's get your mother and go on home."

Discussion

Although this story is my creation, it is, of course, based on the Popeye The Sailor Man Comics characters created by Elzie Crisler Segar, whose Popeye trademark is now owned by King Features Syndicate, Inc., a TM Hearst Holdings Inc.

This is a classic demonstration of the story of David versus Goliath, the underdog who battled against all odds and believed he would prevail. (1 Samuel 17) God loves those who act with a definite and unwavering belief that he is there with them to fight against evil forces. This was David's story: a boy who used a rock and slingshot to down Goliath, the most feared giant warrior, when the other Israelite soldiers were too scared to go near him.

Another uncanny thought about the Popeye character is that his strength came with eating spinach. In the Bible, the prophet Daniel knew how eating foods grown from the earth made him healthier than eating at the Babylonian king's table every night. He proved this by eating nothing but vegetables and drinking only water for ten days. When the ten days were over, Daniel and the other Israelites who went in on the test, were fitter and more well nourished than any of the young men who ate the king's royal foods. (Daniel 1)

Granted, Popeye didn't only eat vegetables, much less only spinach, but it was spinach that gave him his super powers.

The Ocean Blue

Delve into the ocean blue,
submerging within the hue of
sky diamonds misting
through the atmosphere,
swirling around the shade of
sapphire spilling from a
painter's procured palette.

Plummet the depth of
God's comforting hands
and sin's scathing grasps,
collapsing deep into the
cerulean stillness of
awareness and anticipation,
attaining nothing but a
resounding measure of God's love.

Like Swimming in the Ocean

It's like swimming in the ocean,
where the tides course through
and around your skin,
lifting and carrying you
from one end of night to the next.
Waves wrap around the torso,
lifting the chest, caressing thighs.
Currents spin the mind
and you close your eyes.

A touch from a ripple
lingers at the circle on your hand
where you accepted this life's union,
even while fear remained
embraced in your heart.

Then came the time
when you let go of fear and dove
into the enraptured motions.
Promises agreed upon
and proclaimed to God
are exalted by the single rhythm
of two hearts undulating
with the pitch and swell of the sea.

THE LESSON

She could not be this frustrated already. Benjamin just barely woke up. Sandra figured she had waited long enough, with his third birthday party being three weeks ago. She was ashamed that her Benjamin seemed to be the only child still in diapers. A baby really. Sandra looked at his sullen face peering up at her like she was a warden keeping guard over his cell.

When he knew he held her attention, he stood up again! Against her will, she sighed heavily and sat him back down on the potty, a little harder than she intended. *This is the tenth time already*, she thought. *Ten times I sat his narrow butt back down on the potty in the last fifteen minutes, and there hasn't even been a small drop.*

Last week Sandra asked his pediatrician if she could make Benjamin drink a lot of liquids before starting his lesson again. Her few misguided attempts at potty training him in the past, she realized, failed not only because she wanted Benjamin to remain a baby, but because she truly did not have the patience for this. Anger built inside her, taking over her nurturing role, causing her to become a selfish creature whose time was being usurped by this dense child who did not want to learn to use a toilet.

Dr. Liland gave her some pointers, like, "Be patient, and don't give the air that this is so important." And then the kicker. He gave her some titles of books to read on potty training! He's the doctor; why should she pay him to tell her to read and study?

Whatever. She took his few pointers. Patience. Don't say, "Benny, sit the hell down!" Rather, place him nicely back on the potty. Don't say, "You have to learn this to be a normal boy." Rather say, "Mommy has to go potty. Why don't we both try?"

That was twenty minutes ago, and she was near to the point where she longed to yell, "Are you an idiot? Pee, crap, do something, so we can get out of here and I can get far away from you!"

Trying to reclaim her calm, she asked God to please take her anger away and give her some peace. Before she finished with an inward *Amen*, she heard the wonderful sounds of Benjamin grunting out a BM. *Thank you Jesus*, she praised internally.

To Benjamin, she said, "There you go. Knew you could do it," and waited without a celebratory or boastful hurrah and pat on the back for surviving this ordeal. Instead, with a soft smile, she nodded and said, "Now, let's clean you up."

Discussion

It is God's will that parents "do not exasperate your children; instead, bring them up in the training and instruction of the Lord." (Ephesians 6:4 New International Version) Thus, God will help us with patience when we reach out to him.

God also celebrates in our victories, even small ones. Whenever we make an effort to reach out to him for help to better ourselves, he is faithful to help us.

A most well known story delineating God's will to aid us in our victories is that of Solomon. (2 Chronicles 1:7-12) Solomon was a new king of Israel, and anxious about governing God's people righteously. A faithful servant, God wanted to bless him, and in a dream told Solomon he could have anything he asked for. When Solomon asked for wisdom and knowledge to govern God's vast people, it so pleased God that Solomon was granted not only great wisdom, but the worldly possessions he did not ask for, including more wealth than any king before or after him.

The X'es Mark the Spots

Maxine didn't know why she'd dug two holes. It was hard enough to dig one at the depth and width she needed. By the end of the second one, she was exhausted, but she didn't have time to rest before Axel would come home expecting dinner.

While putting away the shovel, Maxine admitted to herself why she made two holes. Alexis would want one too. Although her best friend adamantly discounted Maxine's plan, she was sure that Alexis had enough time to reconsider. Maxine was so sure of this that she knew Alexis' husband Xavier would be with her when she came.

A large, devious smile grew across her face that was in contrast to how unenergetic she felt. But she only had to consider how happy Alexis would be with having a hole too for her to be revived enough to get back to work. There was still a lot to be done.

Several hours later, the dining room table was set for four. Serving dishes of stewed potatoes, honey glazed chicken, and roasted Brussels sprouts and mushrooms filled out the table. Xanthic candle lights ignited the mood she wanted in place when they arrived.

As soon as Maxine dimmed the lights, she heard the keys unlocking the door. Axel was home. Multiple voices and laughter told her that Alexis and Xavier had arrived as well. Maxine's heart drummed, and her hands began to shake with anticipation.

Dinner went without a hitch, and the men were stuffed enough to not put up argument when Maxine demanded their attention. "It's time for your surprise." She gave hand-drawn maps to Axel and Xavier, and continued, "The exes mark the spots. Go look for them now." They began to grumble, until in a stern voice Maxine said, "It's easy and fun. And afterward, apple pie alamode will be waiting for you along with a nice bourbon."

The men quickly snatched up their maps and seemed to hop faster than kangaroos to go out to the backyard. Alexis gave Maxine a knowing smile. It didn't take long for them to hear the first gasps and yelps.

Moments later, the two women gathered their desserts and drinks and made their way outside. Maxine walked over to where she saw Axel laid out perfectly still, and Alexis went around a sturdy gate that separated the spots with their husbands.

Maxine set the dessert and drink on a small table beside the hole she had dug. With a squeal, she jumped into the hole and landed on a luxury mattress made specifically for the depth and width of the hole, and which was delivered and setup an hour before dinner.

Axel rolled over and wrapped himself around Maxine, covering them both up with the down comforter. "You are amazing. This is an unbelievable Father's Day gift."

Maxine smiled and said, "I was glad Alexis' oldest daughter is home to babysit." She looked up at the stars and asked, "So you like it?"

Axel kissed her deeply as an answer. Afterward he said, "Now I'm ready for pie alamode and bourbon."

Discussion

Luckily, there is nothing wrong with a woman attempting to please her husband. A wife's job, even in Biblical times, wasn't just household and motherly duties, but to work as hard as any who loves her family. So says the Bible:

> "She seeks wool and flax, and works with willing hands. She is like the ships of the merchant; she brings her food from afar. She rises while it is yet night and provides food for her household and portions for her maidens. She considers a field and buys it; with the fruit of her hands she plants a vineyard. She dresses herself with strength and makes her arms strong. She perceives that her merchandise is profitable. Her lamp does not go out at night. She puts her hands to the distaff, and her hands hold the spindle." (Proverbs 31:13-19 English Standard Version)

Thus, the modern term of "wonder woman" is not necessarily a new one, as women's work has always gone far beyond what most men have ever considered.

A True Christmas Gift

With eyes closed and wishing for the best,
seven-year-old Anderson instead learned
his parents failed the Christmas Spirit test.

No Christmas lists for Anderson to post,
no lines to Santa to wait expectantly in,
only parents so tired they resembled dreary ghosts.
In the living room, was a skinny fake tree,
which Anderson eyed – it looked as dry as toast.
They failed to notice his tears or his heart so broken,
that he wished Christmas was another time – almost.

The night moved slowly, until he drifted asleep.
Upon waking, he smelled what seemed to be Christmas.
Jumping out of bed, Anderson took a quick leap
down the stairs and, with eyes wide open,
he saw what could only be ...
a true gift of Christmas, not just a token.

In the arms of his mother, looking so small,
was a baby, newborn, cuddled up close.
Turning his head to peer through the hall,
on the dining room table was a Christmas feast
fit for a king, his family and all.

Cinnamon steeped in tea and chocolate,
and stockings hung near a very real tree!
Underneath was a small bassinet.
Did his family suddenly grow
to four from three?

"You came down just in time,"
said Anderson's mother, her voice filled with delight.
"This is your brother, a new heir in our line.
We've adopted him and he needs our love,
so he can learn, as you have so fine,
the true spirit of Christmas."

"What is his name?" Anderson couldn't help but ask.
"You tell us. Look in his eyes and hold him close,
because a name is not something you can remove like a mask."
His father added, "We've been so busy bringing him home.
You're seven years old now, and this is your Christmas task."
Anderson squealed with joy,
"This is the best Christmas day and gift.
This is much better than any old toy."

No more lonely days ahead,
Anderson's seventh Christmas
brought more happiness to his world, instead.

Heat

Smoothly, his hand moves
and glides across my arm,
leaving a trail of humidity in its wake.

Droplets of his heat rise on my skin,
and he takes my hand,
silken and shaken, into his.

Words aren't spoken,
it's time to listen.

The sound of "hush" comes from us both,
quieting the vibrations of our hearts that
diminish our ability to hear.

Our hands meld into one,
knowing this is how it should be.
Our arms draw closer,
our steps align,
and we arrive.

There is nothing left,
but to affirm the commands:
Honor. Love. Keep God with.

Only after, do we vow and alight
in our first kiss as one.

The Other Side

It was the usual ho-hum boring day for Harry Montgomery. Work was the same today as it was yesterday and, undoubtedly, like it would be tomorrow. Harry tried not to be depressed, and silently prayed, *I thank you everyday, God, that I got a job, that I got a wife and a son.*

He tried not to think how going home was no more thrilling than being at work. His wife would be building her farm on the computer, and his son would be crying in the crib, having to wait on his dad to be changed and fed. Steffie felt she did her part at breakfast and lunch.

To boost his spirits, he decided to stop off at 7-11 to get a slushy. He hadn't had a slushy in years.

Harry couldn't wait for two things to happen that would change his life 180 degrees for the better. First, he dreamt of his boy being big enough to play ball, to take long walks, and experience the thrills of nature with him. Harry remembered his own thrill and disgust after he poured out from a rusty can worms he collected for a school science project, planning on placing them in a better container. The worms squirmed and intertwined in a glistening, oscillating ball of flesh.

Second, he imagined his last day at work, walking out of his office as a fully vested retiree!

Harry approached his car, shaking his head as he imagined these two prayers realized. Looking up, he saw a boy who must have been no more than seven holding out a newspaper to him. Behind the boy was a stack of about forty papers.

"Hey boy, this is not the best place to be selling newspapers. Most people when they leave here, they run and won't hesitate for the news."

The boy didn't say anything, which was strange to Harry. His clothes weren't tattered, and Harry believed him not to be homeless. He was likely from the constricting middle-class that was quickly being compressed into the fast growing lower-class. Feeling sorry for him, Harry dug into his pocket, took out the single dollar bill he had in it, and said, "Here, let me have one of those."

The boy looked at the bill, then lifted his hand, palm up and waved it, letting Harry know his offer was too little.

"I tell you," Harry said shaking his head. He scrambled into his wallet and took out two more bills. "Is this enough?"

The boy took the money and gave Harry the paper. Harry laughed to himself, got in the car and, from a quick glance, saw that the newspaper had the date of next week. "Is this some kid's school assignment or prank?" he asked himself aloud.

But the paper looked legit and professional. He opened it from its unbound tri-fold and read the headline story.

"Last week, Harry Montgomery was only minutes too late, having made an unusual stop by a 7-11, and is still trapped outside of the barrier. One of thousands, Harry could do nothing while, on the other side of the invisible and impenetrable barrier, his wife and child now live in what

62

immediately became paradise. His son, no longer an infant, is like all who were babies on that side of the barrier: ten years older.

"In that isolated utopia, there is no need for work or electricity. There are no banks within its borders, and no need for currency. There is, however, a bountiful garden abutting a portion of forest at the edge of the barrier. It is a beautiful landscape of greenery and waterfalls that only God could have created."

Harry stared blankly for a fraction of a second, imagining in a lifetime's worth of details, his two prayers reaching their completion. Immediately, he dropped the paper and in a near trance rushed home, arriving only minutes before the barrier sealed shut.

Discussion

To me, this story is about second chances and having a fresh start. The Bible is all about being given second, third and more chances, as was told to Peter when he asked how many times must he forgive his brother. Jesus responded, not seven, but seventy times seven times. (Matthew 18:21-22) But that's more about forgiving than second chances.

For giving second chances, I have to go to the woman at the well. While resting at a well during his travels from Judaea to Galilee, Jesus began speaking to a Samaritan woman. During their talks, Jesus told the woman to get her husband. She answered that she had no husband. Jesus responded, "You are right when you say you have no husband. The fact is, you have had five husbands, and the man you now have is not your husband. What you have just said is quite true." (John 4:1-18 New International Version)

Yes, Jesus does call us out of our sins, but the point of this was to convict the woman of her sinful and unfulfilling life. By believing in Jesus, by drinking of the living spiritual water of God, she would never thirst again. Instead, the water provided by Jesus would become in her "a spring of water welling up to eternal life." (John 4:14 NIV)

Because of the woman's testimony about her encounter with Jesus Christ, for two days many Samaritans went to speak with him and believed in the living water. (John 4:39-42)

My Boaz

While lying out on my bed, I began to imagine what it would be like when God's promise was fulfilled and I would have my own Boaz as my husband. Without feeling ashamed, I began wondering whether God understood the magnitude of this imagining. I paused and looked out the window at the leaves glowing in the bright sunlight. How far should I go with this?

My Boaz would be a big man, tall and not a skinny thing, handsome of course, at least to me, and funny. He'd be protective, though not overly so, watching over me like Boaz did Ruth. He'd let me be myself. (Most people knew I could be opinionated, though not overly so.) He'd be passionate, but not too outgoing that I'd feel insecure. Family and church would be very important to him, also taking care of me financially, emotionally....

"Okay, Lord, I'll stop there. I don't want to make you blush."

I sat up. I was dressed, but not sure if I was going anywhere. I needed to go to the library, but would also be okay with staying home and watching TV. I had some shows I wanted to catch up on, and there were usually some decent movies on.

"How can I lead you to your Boaz if you're staying home all the time?"

That was a jolt. I knew it was God's voice, and I started to get a little excited. Then I remembered some of those Bible stories. You know the ones, like where Joseph was in prison for umpteen years before God's promise of him becoming ruler came true. And poor old Abraham having to deal with his wife's impatience, not to mention his own, before he finally had a child by her at the age of 100. Then there was David, who had been blessed as the next king of Israel, which didn't happen for about another fifteen years. Oh, I was sure there were many, many more stories like that.

I slowly stood up, not wanting to bank on wasting God's promise, even if it would take another two, eight, twenty years. "Come on now, God, I know you are not expecting me to wait that long. What would I be able to do with my Boaz at sixty-four?"

I could feel God's teasing smile, and knew he was giving nothing away. Deciding on following God's lead, although there was no doubt beforehand, I sauntered into the living room and switched up my slippers for my shoes.

On the way to the car, I started to think of God's other promises that had yet to come to completion. I definitely had pounds to lose, and I was sure he'd said I'd become my ideal weight. Maybe some of that non-fulfillment was my fault too. Not that I was admitting me being without my Boaz was all on my plate.

Then there was my book. Whether being on the New York Times bestseller list was part of his promise, I could not be sure. But undoubtedly, it was God who had me to write it as it was, with just the right amount of intrigue, suspense, darkness and hope. And yes, God won at the end.

At my car, I still hadn't decided where I was going. I had my laptop and could make my way to the library or to a café. In either place there was free Wi-Fi and I could check on the dating site, if I felt like it. I had no hope in that and only joined it at the nagging of my mother, and my friend had joined first.

I started the car with the taste of a chai tea latte imagined on my tongue, and headed towards Starbucks. Thinking of that online site and all the failed potentials in the past, I said, "God, you made them, and I'll say you gave me that craving to want one. So, why is it so darned hard to find one for me? I'm waiting, you know I am, on one of your choosing so as not to be miserable. Do I still have that much to learn?"

God didn't answer, and I refrained from thinking he was just being stubborn. Then a bunch of pictures appeared before my eyes. They were transparent, so there was no risk of me crashing. But maybe then I'd meet a paramedic. My mom would be happy with me meeting someone with that job.

The pictures that popped up were of the many single, wonderful women I knew who were either divorced or never married. Was this supposed to tell me something? I felt it proved my point more than anything else. Slightly indignant, and with some sarcasm, I said, "That just proves my point, God. Where are the men for your chosen women?"

As I parked in the Starbucks' parking lot, I received a murmur of an answer, "For a man to take the place of me for my chosen, he must be developed. Boaz was not created in a day, and neither was Ruth."

I didn't say anything because I understood what he was saying. So, for the time being, I put the imaginations of my Boaz out of mind and went inside with my laptop, sat at a table with my chai tea latte and began to write.

Discussion

The beautiful and romantic story of Ruth and Boaz is in Ruth 2-4.

Whether this piece is fiction or memoir, though there is more fact than imagination in it, Psalms 27:14 says to "Wait on the Lord: be of good courage, and he shall strengthen thine heart: wait, I say, on the Lord." (King James Version) My talks with God when I'm feeling weary, in doubt, frustrated, angry, down, impatient, do give me that good courage to wait on him. Of this, I am very thankful.

Many people do not understand the blessing we have to be able to talk with God and to receive answers. Sometimes those answers come immediately, other times not, but he always hears and comforts if we listen. Abraham understood this. God spoke to Abraham many times, revealing promises, blessings, and directing him to where he should go and when. (Genesis 12:1-9)

It is also important to know that Abraham spoke to God as well. One example was when Abraham bargained with God in an attempt to save Sodom and Gomorrah, asking for them to be spared if there were fifty righteous people among the wicked. Upon Abraham's continued pleading and bargaining, God eventually agreed to spare the land if there were ten righteous people.

Unfortunately, upon sending angels to the land, God learned that, besides Lot and his family, only great evilness prevailed in the people's heart. (Genesis 18-19)

~ A Final Passage ~

The Night Sky

I soar into the night sky,
while the thundering waves below
echo my fears of what lie ahead
and magnify the exhilaration
that I'm soaring with my God,
from and into His creation.

The chill of the night filters
through me as if I were as malleable
as the ocean mist,
while the crashing sound of the waves
speaks to me of God's soothing promises:

"Keep going. Faith will carry you
on your path. The universe
is but a speck of the power that I
have given you. Your tears
evoked from the faithfulness of your
life are love songs to me. Because of
your devotion and trust, the mysteries and
powers of the night sky and all of its
stars and galaxies and worlds unknown to you
are nothing compared to the gift of life
I have given you."

I soar through the night sky,
in the energy of God's ocean,
in the magnetism and density of
all that is His, feeling the power of
His love and the flowing of His promises.

Peering through the open window
into the night sky of His eyes,
I fall asleep to the lullabies of the
thundering and crashing waves of His voice,
and dream of His whispered promises
of tomorrow.

Post Note

The photos within, other than those indicated below, were obtained online and utilized with the belief and intention that they are public domain images. The photos for *A Child of the World, A Child of God Reborn, Like Swimming in the Ocean,* and *A Final Passage* were taken by or of me.

I hope you have enjoyed this collection of my spiritual growth as a writer as well as the discussions, and I welcome any comments made in love. You may contact me via email at: nlarondajohnson-author@yahoo.com.

Please feel invited to give your honest review of *Salted With Fire* on Amazon.com and Goodreads.com. I also invite you to log on to and join the blog "Writer's Mark – Christian and other fiction, poetry and ideas" at: www.nancylarondajohnson.blogspot.com.

About the Author

Nancy LaRonda Johnson is a passionate writer of Christian and other fiction and poetry. She has written short stories, poetry and personal journals most of her life, and has a Bachelor of Arts degree in Sociology and a Juris Doctorate.

Her first book, the literary Christian speculative novel, *Anticipation of the Penitent*, reached the finals in the Indie Publishing Contest sponsored by the San Francisco Writer's Conference 2012, and is receiving high acclaim. She is working on several projects, including a sequel to *Anticipation of the Penitent*. *Salted With Fire* is her second publication.

www.ingramcontent.com/pod-product-compliance
Lightning Source LLC
Chambersburg PA
CBHW040742250626
47164CB00001BA/1